For the one who makes me laugh. . .

who shares my dreams. . .

the one I call "friend."

To

From

On This Date

WHY YOU'RE

My

FRIEND

by Kelly Williams

A DayMaker Greeting Book

WE ALL HAVE FRIENDS WHO COME AND GO THROUGHOUT OUR

LIVES. ON OCCASION, WE'RE BLESSED ENOUGH TO COME ACROSS A

"FOREVER" FRIEND—A FRIEND WHO STAYS FOR A LIFETIME. . .

THROUGH JOYS AND SORROWS, LAUGHTER AND TEARS. THIS LITTLE

VOLUME IS A HEARTFELT REMINDER OF OUR SPECIAL FRIENDSHIP.

Thank you for being my forever friend.

Never shall I forget the days

I spent with you. Continue

to be my friend as you will

always find me yours.

Ludwig van Beethoven

You're my friend

because. . .

You bring sunshine,
laughter, and joy into my life.

You have a special way
of turning the ordinary and mundane into
extraordinary and fun.

You lend unwavering support
in all of my realistic
(and not-so-realistic) endeavors.

You are my source of inspiration.

You encourage my creativity—
no matter how zany my ideas may seem.

You are a beautiful person—

inside and out.

You bring a smile to my

face on the bluest of days.

You willingly listen to my endless chatter. . .

(even when I'm not making any sense).

You have a forgiving heart.

*Your kindness
and warm spirit are contagious.*

We share an unbreakable trust.

You always know just what I need

when I'm feeling low.

On days when I'm feeling
especially unsure of myself,
you remind me of my importance
and contribution to the world. . .

and on days when I'm feeling
less than attractive, you lift me up. . .
until I feel beautiful again.

You approach every task
with zeal and enthusiasm. . .

and you aren't intimidated
by life's obstacles.

You hold my hand when I'm scared. . .

🌀

You hug me when I cry. . .

🌀

You give me advice when I need it. . .

🌀

You sit with me in silence when I don't.

You're always the first one there
when I need a friend.

You look at the positive side
of every situation.

You share everything with me
(even if it's your last piece of chocolate!).

You have taught me to find joy
and meaning in the simple things.

You make me happy
(just because you're you!).

You always offer an honest opinion—
even if it's not what I want to hear. . . .

You are passionate about your beliefs.

You're full of surprises. . .never predictable.

You know how to have fun.
(And you're the only person who can
make me laugh until my stomach hurts!)

You have faith in me,
always encouraging me to follow my dreams.

٩

When I achieve my goals or overcome a challenge,
you celebrate with me. . .

٩

and when I face hardship and disappointment,
you hurt with me, too.

*We can speak
volumes without
any words.*

🌀

*We have a unique
and genuine
understanding of
one another.*

You accept me for
who I am. . .

and you ignore my
annoying habits.

You are generous and thoughtful. . .
often bringing me little gifts
for no special reason but "just because."

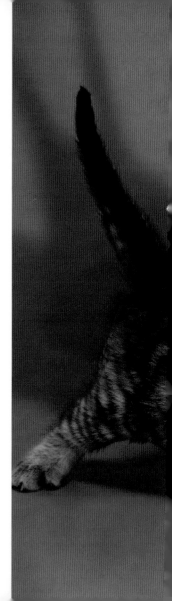

You keep your promises—always.

In your presence I find comfort and peace.

I miss you when we're apart.

No matter how much time goes by. . .
we can always pick up where we left off.

You bring out the best in me—really, you do!

You encourage me to try new things.

And you always bring out
the adventurer in me,
even when I'd rather hide out at home.

You never forget me on my birthday. . .
or any special day.

We have numerous "remember when's"
that make me smile every time
those memories come to mind.

You are patient with me when I'm difficult.

*And you continue to be my friend
when I'm being most unfriendly.*

You pray for me (and I pray for you).

You help me stay focused on days
when I'd rather be daydreaming.

◉

You have taught me to relax
when life's stresses are pressing upon me.

◉

You gently remind me to forget about yesterday's blunders. . .
and help me look forward to tomorrow's opportunities.

◉

When life gets hectic, you are my reality check.

On the busiest of days, you still make time for me.

*You motivate me to go on
(when I'd rather stay in bed than face a new day).*

*Because of you, I never feel lonely,
forgotten, or insignificant.*

You are the most loving person I know.

You are my forever friend.

A friend loves at all times.

PROVERBS 17:17

DayMaker
GREETING BOOKS

© 2004 by Barbour Publishing, Inc.

ISBN 1-59310-201-1

Designed by Kirk DouPonce,
UDG | DesignWorks, Sisters, Oregon

All Scripture quotations, unless otherwise indicated, are taken from the HOLY BIBLE, NEW INTERNATIONAL VERSION®. NIV®. Copyright © 1973, 1978, 1984 by International Bible Society. Used by permission of Zondervan Publishing House. All rights reserved.

Published by Barbour Publishing, Inc., P.O. Box 719, Uhrichsville, Ohio 44683, www.barbourbooks.com

*Our mission is to publish and distribute inspirational products
offering exceptional value and biblical encouragement to the masses.*

Member of the
Evangelical Christian
Publishers Association

Printed in China.
5 4 3 2 1